About

Pregnancy is such a complex experience that varies significantly from woman to woman. It can be extremely challenging, heartbreaking, emotional, and physically depriving, but within the same breath, it is so gratifying and fulfilling, to a point where your heart swells to every nook possible within your chest. The images alongside the stories within the book tell each woman's personal experience within their stage of pregnancy. These are unmasked stories of pregnancy from seasoned mothers, mothers to be, and mothers to babies who are angels and no longer with us. This book is about women harnessing the raw narrative of pregnancy and shaping it into beautiful, truth-telling legacy.

To my everythings;
you were the rock
you were the inspiration.

The majority of the photographs are taken by Nadia Aldea,
unless otherwise stated.

Photographs and each story were offered and used with
permission from photographer and/or the author.

Complete gratitude and appreciation. Thank you for contributing your beautiful images.

Photographs on page 6-7,10-11,188-191 offered by Carling Stiksma
Photograph on page 24 offered by Jamie Sullivan
Photograph on page 50-51 offered by Carley Mendes, of Oh Baby Nutrition
Photographs on page 74, 100 offered by Tami
Photographs on page 104–107 offered by Annabel Clark
Photographs on page 108, 160, 234 offered by Tanya
Photograph on page 110 offered by Nicole
Photographs on page 126-127, 136 offered by Kelly Allen
Photograph on page 138-139 offered by Charlotte Green
Photograph on page 162-163 offered by Katya Nova
Photographs on page 164-166 offered by Laura Ann Photography
Photographs on page 168-169 offered by Emma Collins, of Eskimo Rose Photography
Photographs on page 170–171 offered by Amy Ortega
Photograph on page 186-187 offered by Jill Coursen Photography
Photograph on page 242 offered by Bethany Green Photography

We are all in this together.
Let's support each other.
Let's connect, recharge, and heal.
Your story matters, you matter, and you're not alone.

To all the women who have shared their stories.
This book would not have been possible without you.

Your willingness to share a part of yourselves in hopes of helping others has been astonishing to witness. You've made me cry, smile, laugh, and catch my breath. You've challenged me to grow and have made me feel a part of something so special. THANK YOU.

Major gratitude to my husband for his belief in me, and for always challenging me with your questions and perspectives. To family and friends for your support and continued encouragement.

This has been a beautiful journey.

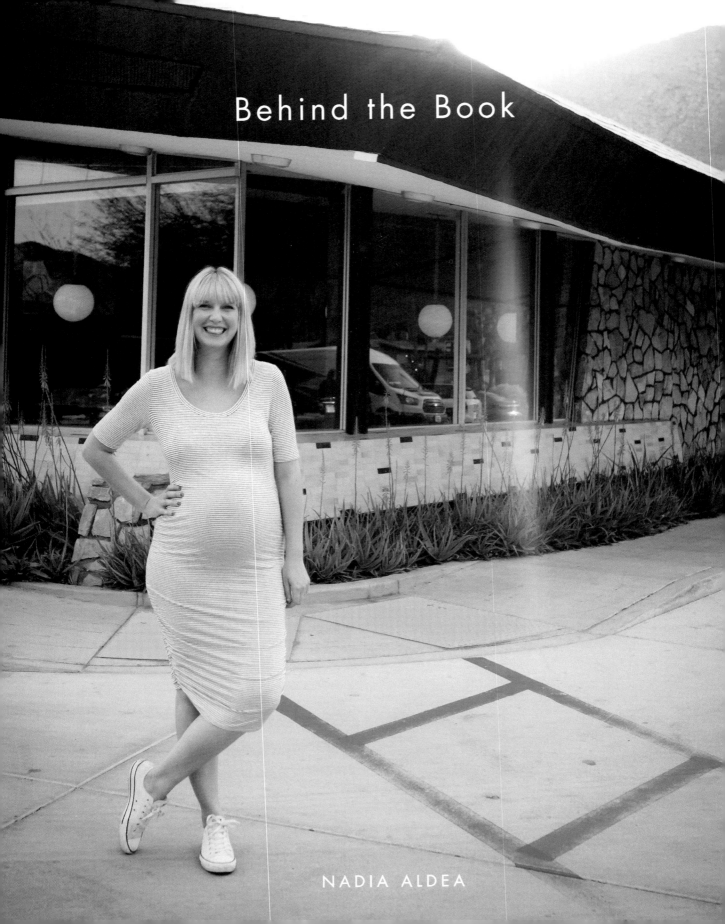

Behind the Book

NADIA ALDEA

A creative deep thinker, a photographer, a proud mama, and self-proclaimed stubborn wife. I approach life with the firm belief that we all have stories to tell, and I feel the most fulfillment and joy when I can help others tell them.

Using two creative avenues, photography and storytelling, *Dear Baby Stories* was born. It's about giving womens pregnancy stories a space to do what honesty and sharing does best: empowering others.

Inspiration for this book came after my first pregnancy with my son. While working on the book, our family was blessed with a second pregnancy, a baby girl. I have shared my own pregnancy stories from two different trimesters. I am honoured to be in the mix with the fascinating women among these pages. Please enjoy these stories; I hope they bring you peace, open your mind, or simply brighten your day.

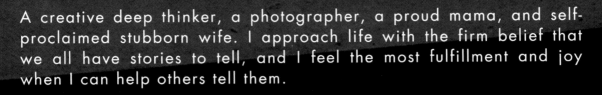

FIRST TRIMESTER
0 to 13 weeks

NADIA, 4 weeks
Edmonton, AB, Canada

"First time we were trying for our first son, it was a monthly disappointment and heartbreak for 9 months. Any woman who tries even for a month knows that heart-wrenching feeling- it takes just even one month of a unsuccessful pregnancy to hurt. The very deliberate way I took the pregnancy test was almost as a sacred ritual; it would be the first time I'd see the positive sign and it needed to happen the best way possible.

This time around I found out alone in a restaurant bathroom, this time around my husband found out via a surprising but calm phone call, this time around I didn't hyperventilate and cry. It was a surreal and alone and calm moment, finding out in such a surprising way, and containing it in me for the night.

This time it is SO different."

JENNY M, 5 weeks
Edmonton, AB, Canada

"We were excited and sad at the same time. We were sad our 14-month-old daughter was being robbed of her "babyhood." But obviously we were so happy to be expanding our family. The next day when I booked a doctor appointment, I had to wait almost two weeks to be seen. I went and got all the prenatal papers, blood work, and vitamins. Two days later I woke up at 5am with slight cramping and a little bit of blood. I panicked and called Health Link. I was told to go to the emergency in the next few hours. I called in sick to work and waited for my daughter to wake up. At 7:30am I packed her up and dropped her off at her Dayhome and met my mother at the ER.

After I arrived I was bleeding quite a bit. I had blood work done and a regular and internal ultrasound, then the doc came to me in the hallway of the hospital and handed me a package from the early pregnancy loss clinic and said,

"I'm sorry, this is a confirmed miscarriage".

I went home and cried for a few hours then picked my baby up and took the next few days to rest. I had to get blood work every 48 hours to make sure my HCG levels were dropping. After my first appointment the pregnancy loss clinic called to inform me that my levels were rising. I was blown away! What does that mean? I did this a few more times and both times the lady called me and said the same thing. They booked me an ultrasound. My mother met me at the lab and the lady requested that we not ask her any questions because of the situation and that the radiologist would speak to us when she finished. When she was done with her pictures, she turned the screen to us and said, "Here is the baby, and there is baby's heartbeat! Congrats!" My mom and I started bawling-- it was quite the scene. I knew there was a baby in me still, and I knew the ER doc was wrong.

I had to continue the blood work, and each time my levels went up. I had to do a follow-up ultrasound, and I chose to go by myself this time because everything was okay. My baby had a heartbeat and it would be fine. I briefed the woman doing the ultrasound on situation, almost in a cocky way, like I knew more then the silly doc who said I had a miscarriage. She did the exam and when I asked her if the heartbeat was good, she dodged my question. She left the room to grab the radiologist for about four minutes. Four longest minutes of my life.

I had an anxiety attack. I got dizzy and really felt like I was going insane. The radiologist came in and said "do you know where this is going" I muttered that I had a good guess. He said I'm sorry your baby no longer has a heart beat and hasn't grown since last weeks ultrasound.

That was it. I didn't cry. I got dressed and fought back my tears and got in my car. I took a few to process what just happened. This is now my second time in two weeks that I've been told I'm miscarrying, and now this is the real confirmation. There's no more baby. I finally felt peace. This pregnancy was unfortunate from the beginning and now I can breathe and stop feeling like a crazy person. I got prescribed Misoprostol to take care of the remains stuck in body, and I'm terrified to take them. I have arranged for friends and family to help me and baby over the next few days. I just wish I could fall asleep and wake up tomorrow with everything taken care of and no more sadness or what ifs and whys."

• • • • •

"She did the exam and I asked her if the heartbeat was good, she dodged my question. She left the room to grab the radiologist for about four minutes. Four longest minutes of my life."

MEGHAN, 6 weeks
Canmore, Alberta, Canada

Dear Baby, I've only recently found out that you're on your way, hopefully growing inside me. I'm so excited for you, you're my next dream, you'll complete our family. I'm also so nervous and scared for you. After two miscarriages, I now enter pregnancy with cautious apprehension. Nothing would make me happier than to have you grow into a beautiful child.

I know there's a normal chance that that will happen, but there's a very large part of me though that knows that might not happen and that makes me so sad. You have two brothers or sisters that none of us will ever meet. I know their spirits will go on and become babies for someone else, or maybe they'll even come back through you. I've let them go now. I'm hoping I won't have to say goodbye to you too soon as well.

Your one older brother that you will meet is wonderful and I know he'll be an amazing big brother. He's so loving and sweet. Your Daddy is wonderful too, he's a great Dad already and will be for you as well. I know there's nothing you or I can do to make sure you do continue to grow. You're in the hands of uncontrollable powers. But just know that you are already loved and if you do stay with us, there is a wonderful world out here full of people who love you and we are so excited to show it all to you. Love, Your Mommy.

. . . . .

ELIZABETH, 8 weeks
Edmonton, AB, Canada

"Emily would lay on me and kiss my belly only up until week 7, and a week later I found out the baby had stopped growing.

A loss is a loss, no matter at what stage. A woman who has a miscarriage feels it on an intuitive very raw level.

The sooner you accept it, the sooner you stop blaming yourself, the sooner you can start healing, the sooner you're able to move on."

. . . . .

JOANNA, 8 weeks
Edmonton, AB, Canada

"I couldn't wait, so I ran into the bedroom where he was still sound asleep. I was crying and breathing so loudly that I woke him up. He screamed 'what happened?!' looking like I gave him a heart attack, and I said loudly through the tears 'I am pregnant!'.

I am slowly starting to feel better about everything. I am still terrified, but just feeling more like I will find my own way as a mom and we will find our own way as a family and things will just work out because they have to."

• • • • •

JAMIE, 8 weeks
British Columbia, Canada

"My hope for you, reader, if you should ever find yourself 'here,' or if by perfect chance you too have lived through your own version of fear and loss, is this: may you find a friend in your fears, a life-sustaining fire in your heart, and the quiet comfort in the idea that someone is 'there,' strong in spirit, with you.

This poem (Poem 1) comes from the day before my first ultrasound. I already knew in my body this babe was not staying. I had gone from ecstatic perfection in my life (a life I worked hard and lovingly to create) to shock and terror about my potential future.

I knew something was 'wrong.'

I had just gotten married that Christmas Eve, my husband's business was growing and so was mine, and we were happy, in love, and proud about all the hard work we'd done following our hearts and taking risks to live a truly satisfying life. We had a beauty-filled Christmas, full of merriment and laughter - and discovered we were finally pregnant (after three long years of patiently waiting) on Boxing Day.

Poem 1

Help me see and help me be
Dear roots grow deep
Eyes rise up - see me from the safety of the sky
I am a body of more than flesh and blood.
Wise and observant
Not shaken not stirred
Holding on to what is holy.
Command from me faith and trust
I am Ready - Terrified and Unsure
Now is the time.
Dear me, mimic the giant boulder on the ground / come
down from the stars in the far away moonlit sky.
With the mother's heart that
now beats inside of me
I have no choice but to face
this very personal potentiality
I Am the Mother, I always have been - fierce like fire and
strong like the glowing sun
Yet here melted into this moment,
so very raw & delicate –
I am likened to a single
snowflake caught on my warm finger-

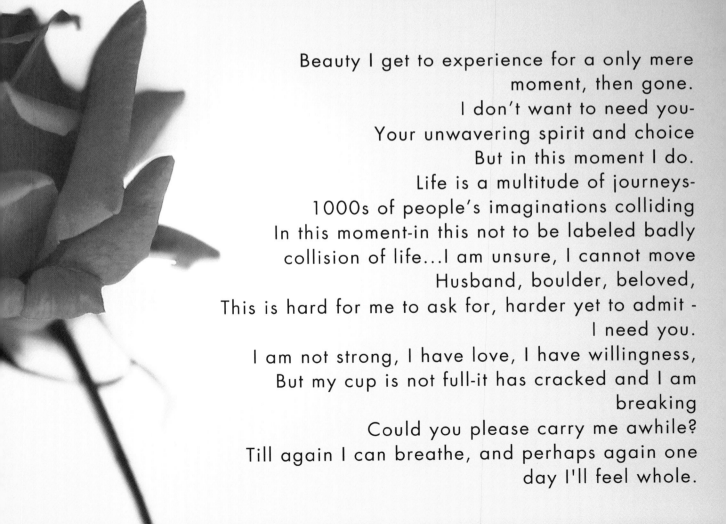

Beauty I get to experience for a only mere
moment, then gone.
I don't want to need you-
Your unwavering spirit and choice
But in this moment I do.
Life is a multitude of journeys-
1000s of people's imaginations colliding
In this moment-in this not to be labeled badly
collision of life...I am unsure, I cannot move
Husband, boulder, beloved,
This is hard for me to ask for, harder yet to admit -
I need you.
I am not strong, I have love, I have willingness,
But my cup is not full-it has cracked and I am
breaking
Could you please carry me awhile?
Till again I can breathe, and perhaps again one
day I'll feel whole.

Poem 2

Written 5 days after my surgery
to remove my child and my
fallopian tube from my body,
and from this living world.

Tell me who you are right now.

I can't.
I don't know.
I am a million shades of blue.
I am a thousand flowers-picked before they could bloom.
I am the aches and pains of old women everywhere who've endured through
the decades the depths of death.
I am all the strong virile men-who must stand by and watch without control.
I am a new mother's heart,
Shattered by loss-
Trillions of pieces blowing endlessly like gypsies in the wind-never to settle.
I am a yearning to rest in what once was whole.
I am intense hurt.
I am unyielding pain.
I am an awakening.
I am a tired spirit-ready for rest in the arms of my husband's broken heart.

MY TURN.

You are the strength you do not yet know.
You are the infinite-
Always changing – therefore always the same.
You are the perfection of every sunrise.

You are the calming completion of every finished day.
You are a shining marvel existing with no necessary purpose.
You are beautiful.
You are still FULLY a Woman.
You have TIMELESS value.
You are the other.
You are yourself.
And I am you.

...An endless fountain of untapped Love."

• • • • •

LINDSAY, 9 weeks
Edmonton, AB, Canada

"Well. So here we are. 9 weeks along. It's going by quickly this time! I'm not sure if I've even fully digested the fact that my sweet baby girl Mercy will be a big sister.

It's hard to wrap my head around the fact that there will be another living, breathing, tiny bundle of pure joy in our house.

Another child to love, to care for, to nurture, to guide. It's such a huge responsibility, and an honor for which I am humbled. I am brought to my knees daily in prayer and adoration for the sheer magnificence of creation, of life itself. The fact that the Creator Himself has chosen ME, has specially selected ME of all His children, to carry yet another miracle of life into His kingdom."

• • • • •

ELYSE, 9 weeks
Oklahoma, USA

"Having our first baby was wonderful! There is nothing on this earth like carrying a child, and the overwhelming love you can have for someone that you have never met. I myself have loved several sweet angels without ever meeting them.

...After years (almost 5) of trying for baby number two, and not without some truly emotional trials, it finally happened. My story is one of comfort, but also one of loss.

In April of 2011, my father went into the ICU. I think we as a family all knew that this time was approaching due to my father's declining health over the years. I was especially close to my father and was certainly a daddy's girl. My dad was in the ICU on and off life support for over 3 weeks before he had passed. I was at the hospital every chance I could get. One day, my whole family was in the hospital visiting my dad. We received some bad news as to my dad's worsening condition, so we had decided to take a walk down the hall.

As I was walking, I kicked something on the floor. I reached down to pick it up, and as I realized what it was I immediately started crying. I picked up what looked like a charm off a bracket. It was an angel charm with the word "faith" on it. If that's not a sign from God, I'm not sure what is!! That isn't the most crazy thing that had occurred. That night as I lay sleeping, I had the most vivid dream I've ever had; I dreamt about my dad. In the dream, he had told me that everything was going to be alright and that God had bigger plans for me.

He explained that the only way for me to have another child was for him to go with God.

In my dream I pleaded with him, but according to him the plan had already been made. About two days later on Easter morning, my father passed away. I had told my husband and my sister about the dream, and hadn't thought too much into it at the time. Truly believing it was some unconscious truth to my dream.

However, around 9 weeks later, I discovered that I was in fact pregnant. I looked at my husband and we immediately thought the same thing! After years of trying for another baby and having loss after loss....we were finally able to bring a sweet little boy into this world! We named him after my dad!"

• • • • •

"…your dad and I were in complete awe of you. We already adore you more than you will ever know."

SHAY'LE, 11 weeks
Texas, USA

"At your first ultrasound I was about 11 weeks along. We made sure Dad was home for it. It was the most amazing thing to see you, so tiny on that screen. We could see your head, belly, arms/hands, legs/feet. You were sleeping at first, and then you woke up and started squirming around, kicking your legs and punching your arms. It was funny, precious, and your dad and I were in complete awe of you. We already adore you more than you will ever know. I can promise you that you are already the center of our world; our world already revolves around you. We will do anything and everything in our power to provide for you and give you a wonderful life."

JENNY L, 11 weeks
Edmonton, AB, Canada

"I learned from my last pregnancy that nothing is in my control. So I am hoping to be more laid back, go with the flow and accept things as they come.

I want for this baby to be calm and content. Sylvie was VERY active, aware, and colic. I felt so terrible that I could not comfort her. She is very happy now but for the new baby, as an infant, I hope they are comfortable and content.

I look forward to loving someone as much as I love Sylvie. It seems impossible to me at the moment but the idea of feeling that much love is overwhelming and amazing."

• • • • •

SECOND TRIMESTER
14 to 26 weeks

LISA, 16 weeks
Canmore, AB, Canada

"I have been worried about my identity. Selfish, I know. I am worried that I cannot do the things I want. In the short term, I will need to defer my MBA a year and in the long term, how can I accomplish my big dreams, and how can I pursue my passion with the same rigour when I am a mother?

I was terrified I would be a bad mother. What I have learned is this: children don't do what they are told; they do what they see. If you I want to inspire my child to have self esteem, I need to have self esteem. If I want to inspire my child that they can do whatever they set their mind to, simply telling them will do nothing. If they see me pursue my passion they may just have the courage to do the same.

How dare I use having children as an excuse to not be great. My misconception was that motherhood only looks like one thing when there are as many versions of motherhood as there are mothers. The way it makes sense to me is that I will go out every day to strive to make the world a better place.

I will continue to grow, learn, seek, reach and challenge myself daily, knowing that is what I want to inspire in my children. There is not anything wrong with being 'selfish.' It actually may make you the best role model for your child."

• • • • •

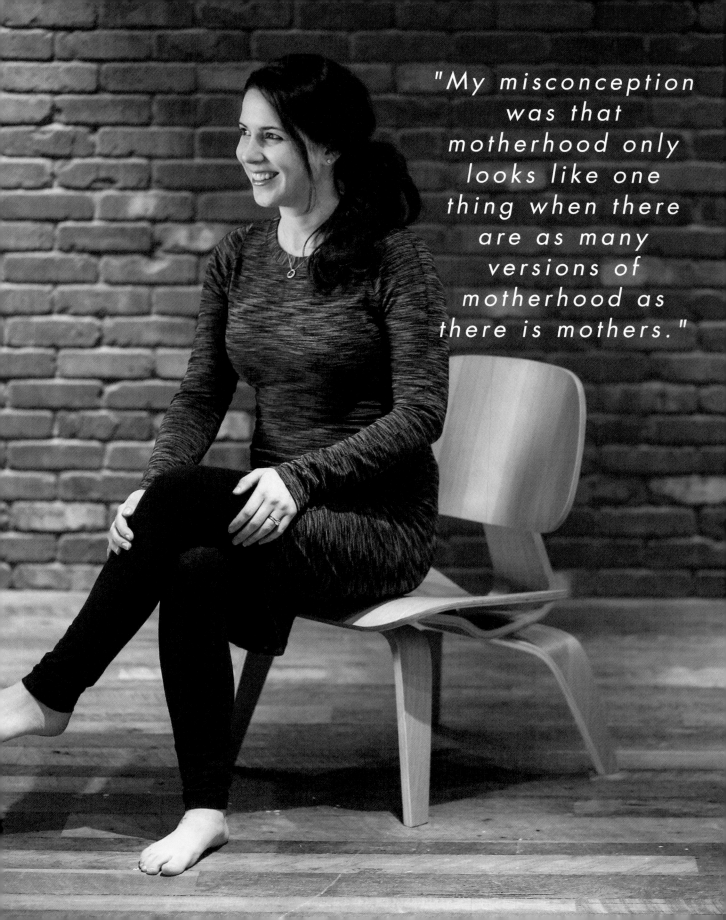

"My misconception was that motherhood only looks like one thing when there are as many versions of motherhood as there is mothers."

CARLEY, 17 weeks
Vancouver, BC, Canada

"It's hard to describe, but along with this little life growing is an incredible energy building inside of me. Sometimes it makes me nauseous; sometimes it makes me giddy. Birthing my first-born was the single most empowering experience of my life. Being witness to the power that nature holds in these moments is extraordinary.

The birth of a child has the ability to change you like nothing else. At the climax of a woman's labor, she will meet her breaking point. She'll feel as though she can't do it, that she just can't go on, and she is right. The maiden in her is not strong enough for the task at hand, and it's during this time that the maiden dies. This happens so that she may be reborn as a mother, with her child. A new, more capable version of herself that has far more strength than she has ever known."

• • • • •

PAMELA, 18 weeks
Edmonton, AB, Canada

"Little did we know, this was not like the others and was going to rock us to our core."

"My husband and I had a relaxed approach on starting our family. With two previous miscarriages both within the first trimester we were slightly apprehensive but optimistic about 'seeing what could happen.' Obviously my first two pregnancies weren't exactly a walk in the park. So naturally, once there seemed to be complications with our most recent one, we weren't surprised. Little did we know, this was not like the others and was going to rock us to our core.

I had began spotting around 12 weeks and ended up in emergency.

*I am very aware of my body, and
I had a feeling things weren't okay.*

The doctor I saw was very compassionate with my history, and decided bed rest and a follow up ultrasound was necessary to ensure things were moving along correctly. I left the hospital feeling great, after hearing and seeing our baby's heartbeat.

I went part-time at work, but I started feeling so much better in the weeks to come leading up to my second trimester.

My follow up ultrasound was in week 14, and aside from the ultrasound technician having a difficult time pinpointing our baby's parts because he/she was very squirmy, I left the appointment feeling great because again-- there was a heart beat and I was almost in the clear and out of the dreaded first trimester.

The next week I saw my OBGYN and I was so excited to ask if I could get back to working more. He told me as long as I was feeling well to go for it. I had my genetic screen the same morning, and the ultrasound seemed fine. I was so happy to see our baby again. Hands and feet and very active. I was elated. Directly after the ultrasound you are expected to have blood work taken directly after.

As I was waiting my turn I received a phone call from the doctor I met in the emergency room. Honestly, it was all a blur. She was telling me she was referring me to the perinatal clinic as the follow up ultrasound showed a blockage in our baby's bladder.

I was so confused. We decided to relax and trust that we had been referred as a precaution and also took comfort in the fact that we had ultrasounds since then and no negative news. The week after was my husband's birthday. That was the day the perinatal clinic called with our appointment for that week.

Trusting that everything was going smoothly, I decided to let my husband head to work, and I would go to the appointment alone.

Once I arrived at the Lois Hole Women's Hospital I was greeted by our high-risk doctor. I hadn't considered us high risk, I didn't even know what that meant. Because again, in my mind, my baby had a heartbeat, which meant it was fine. As I lay down, the doctor began to show me the blockage in our babies tummy. A big, black hole. Still, in my mind I was hopeful, he was moving so much she couldn't even determine the sex. We concluded the ultrasound, as she explained she would need to speak with me in her office. She asked if my husband was here, or if we could call him.

What on earth was going on? She sat me down, and started explaining that the blockage in our baby's tummy was resulting in no fluid being drained and therefore our baby could not develop lungs properly. She then began to explain that they could use a shunt to drain the fluid for the baby, if the baby was male and if there were no genetic disorders diagnosed. Before I knew it, she was convinced our baby had trisomy 18 as this was common in those babies, and my blood work from my ultrasound had markers for that as well.

"The morning of September 5th 2014. Almost 18 weeks. I was told to push. I couldn't. It would be all over if I did."

We tried to call my husband at work. I was devastated. He called, and naturally I was hysterical. I sat outside in the hospital's garden and cried.

The morning of September 5th, 2014. Almost 18 weeks. I was told to push. I couldn't. It would be all over if I did. What would our baby look like? I was petrified at the thought of grieving someone I wanted to know and love so badly. The feeling of having your baby come out of you and not hearing a cry is a thought I still have to blank out to this day. The only comfort I found in that moment was my husband. The room was silent. We spent the next couple of hours holding our son, Hank R.K. Adam. Saying goodbye was torture. Knowing he had suffered, knowing I couldn't make it better was the most despairing feeling I would ever have.

Looking back now, almost a year later, is still so difficult.

I think we are coping the best way we can. We are very blessed and try to remember that whenever we are feeling the loss of Hank. It's still very unbelievable, the process we went through. We find comfort in family and friends. Their little ones add so much joy to our lives.

There is no doubt the last two years of losses has changed the dynamic of our relationship, but I'm fortunate to have been taught the raw vulnerability that came with it. It has made us so much stronger as a pair should we decide to 'try' again.

I wish more understood the pain of pregnancy loss, but at the same time I truly hope women who have loved and lost do not let their experience define them, but instead share their story for others looking for comfort."

• • • • •

KARISSA, 19 weeks
Edmonton, AB, Canada

"When the home pregnancy test came back positive, we were elated, but a feeling of worry and nervousness accompanied the joy. Three months prior to this pregnancy, we lost our first at 6 weeks. Although this pregnancy is progressing well and normally, the worry and fear of miscarriage still haunts me. However, I do my best to move past the fear and celebrate in this new life that grows within me.

I've heard it said that 'you're never REALLY prepared to have kids,' and, at this point, I think it's true. My husband and I planned for this. We had our time frames determined as to when we'd start trying, we put away some money to save for the cost of starting a family and supporting a child, and we felt prepared to step into this new chapter of our lives as parents. After the miscarriage, we were blessed to be able to get pregnant again so quickly. Yet, once it became a reality for the second time, the panic started to set in.

Was this really the right time? Did we have enough money put away? Would we be able to afford to have me stay at home to raise our family after maternity leave benefits run out, or will I go back to work? Did we travel enough? Maybe we should've taken a few more vacations and seen other places before starting a family. It will never really be 'just the two of us' again. It's in those moments of panic that I do my best to re-focus my mind on of all the joy a child and a family can bring. Although there's some uncertainty as to what our lives will look like in the months and years to come, we truly do look forward to having this child and raising our family. We witness the delight and laughter our nephews and nieces bring to our family gatherings - life wouldn't be the same without them!

Pregnancy definitely brings worry and fear, especially after experiencing a loss, but it also brings wonder and excitement!

Being able to feel our tiny child squirm and move is so remarkable and reassuring! Feeling the tiny person we created grow, kick, and play is incredible! Planning the nursery, picking out our diaper bag, and shopping in the baby section have been activities I've really been enjoying. We had our first ultrasound this past week and got our first look at our child. It was so amazing to see how the baby is developing and to watch it shift and move within me. We can't wait to meet this tiny person and thank God for this incredible blessing and His faithfulness through our experiences this far."

• • • • •

FALYNN, 19 weeks
Edmonton, AB, Canada

"Once we decided we wanted to get pregnant, I was unaware of the adventure ahead. After months of trying and some challenges with ovulating regularly, we got pregnant; however, from day 1 something wasn't right. With a mixture of irregular symptoms and nonsensical timing, the doctor refused to say congratulations because the pregnancy wasn't going to last. Turns out, my hormones were unable to sustain the pregnancy and we came to accept the fate; after 7 weeks the demise had officially begun.

Eventually after the miscarriage had run its course, we started trying, yet again. Sure enough, 3 months later, we saw the two pink lines! I had so many apprehensions with the start of this pregnancy, expecting it to end up the same way as my previous; however, after every check-up, things were looking great, at least until 16 weeks when we got the news from our Quad Screening that all my results were substantially elevated and of concern. Considering we hadn't had an ultrasound yet, my doctor sent me for an immediate appointment in order to get a referral to a specialist. So fast forward to 18 weeks pregnant, after a rough first trimester, accepting my rapidly expanding body, the hormone roller-coaster, and the unfortunate news of our test results, we were finally going to see our baby...

Previous to the ultrasound starting, the technician asked us a handful of questions and we explained our situation. So as they do in ultrasounds, she took a look on her screen before showing us the ultrasound. After a minute of her evaluating what she saw, she cautiously turned on our screen and said,

"So there is your baby's head..."
we were in awe, and she followed
it up with, "... and there's your
other baby's head.
Congratulations,
you're having twins!"

So far, they are happy, healthy, and growing perfectly. I think the miscarriage never happened, the baby just wanted a buddy (or a wombmate as we call them)."

• • • • •

#dearbabystories

TAMI, 22 weeks
Oakland County, Michigan, USA

"I wish I had the words. To describe the feelings that I have had today. Instead, I just feel exhaustion. The millions of thoughts, wishes, hopes and dreams that have flooded my head are overwhelming. The tears have been constant. I want so much for you, sweet baby. I want so much for us, as a family. I can't possibly hold you any closer, as you are one with me. Yet I wish to hold you in my arms more than anything. I've been rubbing my swollen belly, feeling your every move. So thankful for your sweet reminders that you are indeed alive and thriving within. You are a mystery in more ways than one. I will love you more than you will ever understand no matter how this mystery ends... I will love you, my sweet baby."

SYLVIE, 22 weeks
Edmonton, AB, Canada

"'This too shall pass!' The frustrating phases are just that - phases. Have patience and wait it out as baby continues to grow and develop. I hope I can keep this in mind with my second."

I've been pregnant before and have a general idea what to expect in that regard. I've brought home a baby, nursed him at all hours of the night, changed diapers, and baby-proofed the house as he learned roll, crawl, walk and now run. I have experience being a mom to a baby, and now a vibrant and active little toddler.

I feel more prepared to be a mom to my second son than I did with my first.

But after needing a scheduled c-section under general anesthesia at 38 weeks with my first son, I have no experience with laboring and delivering a baby.

I feel like my status as second time mom means that I am supposed to know what I'm doing, and have an easier labor and delivery. But my experience in other aspects of being a mom highlights my inexperience in giving birth and makes me more nervous for a VBAC. Conversations with my doula, yoga, and practicing breathing will help me be ready for a successful VBAC with this baby.

I look most forward to meeting my second son. Since he will be my second baby, I am lucky to already know how wonderful it feels to have a newborn fall asleep on your chest and smell their sweet little head. I can't wait to meet him, and see if he looks like his big brother, or like me or his dad."

• • • • •

CHRISTINA, 25 weeks
St. Albert, Alberta, Canada

"Today you were moving lots again and it is starting to feel more weird because you are getting bigger and stronger and starting to move all over the place."

"I want my doctor to give me answers because I worry all the time about every little thing. You will learn that about me when you get older."

· · · · ·

AMANDA, 25 weeks
Edmonton, AB, Canada

"I always thought my life would be a little more set when I started having kids. My career, my home, the city I wanted to live in. No one ever really knows how their life will turn out, but I never imagined I'd be so unhappy pursuing the white picket fence life and how happy I am living the adventure I am on with my husband and our little one on the way.

When we started talking about when to have kids, we didn't know what our life would look like in a year, or even 6 months, but we knew that we wanted a child to be a part of it. I guess you could say that we broke all the rules when it comes to being 'ready' for having kids and just decided to see if God had plans for us to have one anyway.

I hope our little one has so many adventures, with and without his mom and dad, and that he grasps every opportunity that comes his way. We want to teach him to live outside the box, so it makes sense that we would continue to be our entrepreneurial, creative selves as we enter parenthood. It may not be the most predictable path, but it's genuine for us, and we wouldn't have it any other way."

• • • • •

LAURA, 26 weeks
Edmonton, AB, Canada

"Although my first pregnancy, delivery, and recovery was hard with my first I'm so thankful for this pregnancy. Experiencing a loss in between as well makes me wonder about that baby, but also makes me feel so blessed that there is life inside of me! Even though we experienced pain I'm glad we can feel hope as well.

I think that our new family dynamic will be good but busy with two little ones at home. I'm excited to see my daughter grow into her role as a big sister, and I'm excited to see my kids grow up together. I'm excited to become a family of four and to give our little girl a sibling. I'm looking forward to newborn snuggles and holding my baby in my arms."

MAGDA, 27 weeks
Edmonton, AB, Canada

"Learning to take the ups and downs, and the joys and challenges of pregnancy as they come... knowing that for every sleepless night, every stretch mark, every back pain, every cry there will be a little smiling face waiting to meet us."

"I suppose one of the most surprising things about pregnancy is the range of emotions that I find myself going through. We learned early on how fragile pregnancy can be, and I was surprised at how attached I actually was to this little life inside of me. The overwhelming need to provide for and protect our baby has given me a genuine understanding of the unconditional love associated with motherhood. With this has also come a newfound ability to surrender control over my body and my emotions which is not something I ever thought I would be able to do. Learning to take the ups and downs, and the joys and challenges of pregnancy as they come... knowing that for every sleepless night, every stretch mark, every back pain, every cry there will be a little smiling face waiting to meet us.

I hesitate to call it loneliness, but I never imagined that homesickness would be something that I associate with my pregnancy. My husband and I moved to Edmonton last year, leaving behind my family and large group of friends. I have embraced our new life and have yet to experience any real homesickness until now. Not for the place, but for the people. Although I have gained my amazing in laws and new circle of friends, I guess I expected that I would be sharing this experience with my best friends and family nearby. Having said all of this,

I find myself lying awake at night feeling the little kicks in my belly, overcome by gratitude.

Gratitude for my health and the health of our baby, gratitude for the support of our families and friends near and far, gratitude for my amazing husband and soul mate, and gratitude for our situation in life knowing that our little man will come into this world with a warm roof over his head, a safe bed to sleep in and unconditional love from everyone around him."

• • • • •

#dearbabystories

TAMI, 28 weeks
Oakland County, Michigan, USA

"Dearest baby, I wanted to say thank you. Thank you for the last lovely weeks. Your most energetic kicks and tumbles. The beautiful way you have rounded and stretched my body. I've been able to enjoy your presence without daily sickness and I am so grateful I could cry. I'm imagining who you will be. Your coos, your breath, your sweet newborn smell. Oh January, you just can't get here soon enough. Love you my sweet baby."

THIRD TRIMESTER
28 to 40+ weeks

KAREN, 26 weeks
SARAH, 28 weeks
Greenpoint, Brooklyn, New York

"Being pregnant with my sister made the whole experience more magical."

• • • • •

#dearbabystories

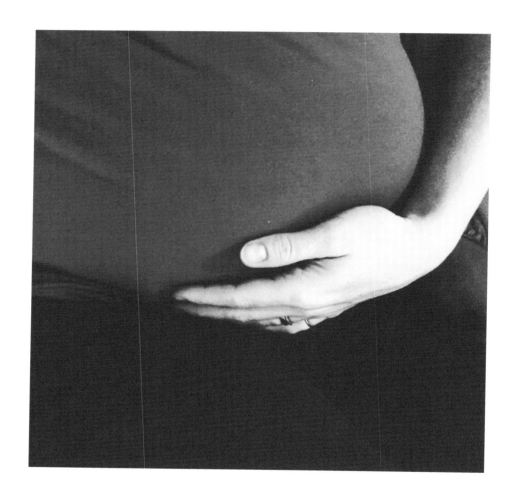

TANYA, 27 weeks
Ann Arbor, Michigan, USA

"My tiny one, I am so thankful I'm getting to know you, how different you already are from your big sister. And, I'm trying really hard, but if I'm being honest, I'm not always embracing all of the changes carrying you keeps placing on my body with the grace I'd hoped. Brutal sciatic pain, pelvic instability, killer heartburn, less-than-ideal sleep over months already, facing down yet another three-hour glucose test in the morning and most likely another diabetic pregnancy brought me to tears I was embarrassed to shed even in front of your daddy tonight. But even if I'm not gracefully 'glowing' and shouting how much I love being pregnant to anyone who listens, none of it changes how grateful I am that we have the promise of knowing you in three more months. I'll do my best to keep you safe and healthy until we meet on the outside, ok? Maybe, just cut your mama a little slack every now and then. And maybe, let's try not to arrive as late as your sister did, k?"

#dearbabystories

NICOLE, 29 weeks
Southern California, USA

"Baby boy is getting big. I keep telling Jordan I can't imagine getting any bigger than this, that this is how far my skin can stretch and it can't take anymore. I still have 10 more weeks to grow. Everything just seems so much... more with this pregnancy.

Maybe my body knows that I had it easy with Molly. That this is our last baby and it wants me to experience everything a pregnancy has to offer, even more so since I got a pass the first time around. These kicks and his hiccups are the last that I will be feeling from the inside. In most cases you don't realize it's the last time till it's too late, but I'm well aware. So while I complain to Jordan about the endless heartburn and midnight leg cramps I'll remember that there are only so many of these left. That one day these little flutters will be a distant memory and start to fade. I'll go from birthing babies to rocking them in my arms, holding them on my hip and sending them off to preschool, elementary, high school and college.

I still have a long way to go till I have an empty nest, but I'm ten weeks away from an empty womb and that's making me feel all the feels today."

MELANIE, 29 weeks
Edmonton, AB, Canada

"My husband and I began trying to get pregnant right after we got married. I was 28, and my husband a few years older and we knew we didn't want to wait long to begin our new chapter. After a couple months of trying, I began to wonder 'what if I can't get pregnant?' That thought haunted me over the next 3 years.

A year into unsuccessful trying, we were referred to the fertility clinic.

We waited 14 months to have our first appointment, and during that time we went for multiple tests, ultrasounds and what seemed like daily blood work. The doctors could find no reason why I was not getting pregnant. At our first specialist appointment, we came up with a plan. We tried 3 rounds of Clomid. It didn't work. 3 rounds of Clomid with IUI. Still no baby. Our doctor was retiring so we met with our new doctor who we instantly loved. He came up with a new treatment plan. He was determined to get us our baby!! In October of 2014 we started a round of injections combined with IUI.

The needles were terrifying and I screamed with each needle I gave myself. It was an expensive and painful experience, but ultimately we wanted a baby so we were willing to do it. My husband cried as he saw my bruised stomach, but knew I would do anything to get us our baby. Injections were followed by more blood work and ultrasounds, and driving to the hospital every 2 days seemed to be our new normal. We were hopeful at the next ultrasound when they told us there were 2 mature eggs!! The nurse told us worst case scenario would be twins! We were ecstatic! 2 weeks later, no baby. I was devastated. The emotional roller coaster was too much for my husband and I to handle. I couldn't handle another month of painful needle and appointments only to be disappointed.

We decided to take a break over Christmas and reevaluate in the new year. During that time we had 9 close friends tell us they were expecting. My world was shattered. I cried a lot. I was genuinely happy for every one of my friends but was trying to come to terms with the possibility of a new normal for my husband and I, a life with just the 2 of us. The thought brought us both to tears. We were so happy together and knew we could be happy if it was just us, but we so badly wanted a family. My husband and I decided we would try one more round, and if it didn't work we would save up and do IVF in the summer.

We wanted our baby!

So we started another round of injections and appointments. The needles were more painful this time but I was determined for it to work!

On January 26th, my 31st birthday, I was scheduled to take my HCG trigger shot. We would go for our IUI 2 days later. So after an evening celebrating with friends, enjoying some great food and wine, we went home feeling hopeful and extremely optimistic! A baby for my birthday? What could possibly be better? I will never forget the day we went in for our IUI. The nurse was so lovely and she saw that my birthday was 2 days before and she said "Let's get you a baby for your birthday!" This time there was only one mature egg so I was cautiously hopeful to avoid disappointment. The next 2 weeks seemed like forever. On Feb 13, 2015, I went in for blood work. I tried so hard to distract myself waiting for the call from the nurse. So I took a nap. At about 4pm we got the call to tell us we were pregnant! I couldn't believe it. I can't even begin to describe the feelings in that moment! I was in shock and filled with tears of joy!

3 years of disappointment each month, and in that moment it seemed like no time had passed!

3 weeks later at our ultrasound we found out we were expecting twins! Another new set of emotions filled both my husband and me!! It was a dream come true!

Our dream was short lived as we went for another ultrasound a few weeks later and found out that our little Baby B did not make it. The baby had stopped growing at about nine weeks. Baby A was healthy and thriving. That was one of the hardest things I have ever had to go through. I was confused, frustrated and angry. I didn't understand why this was happening after all the pain we went through to get pregnant. My husband and I mourned the loss of our baby, while staying strong for our healthy baby that was still growing. The days slowly got easier but little things would still trigger emotion of our angel baby. On May 28th, we found out that we are expecting a Baby Girl!!! It was the happiest day!!

I have dreamed of having a little girl my whole life! Our dream was becoming a reality.

Now we are 11 weeks away from meeting our little princess, and though there are days I still think about our Baby B, I know our little Baby B is in Heaven, and I am thankful for the baby I am still carrying. I cannot wait to be a mom and although the journey has been anything but easy, it has been worth every minute!

I hope that women can find encouragement in my story and can know that no matter how great the battle, the joy that comes when you get through it is so worth it!"

• • • • •

#dearbabystories

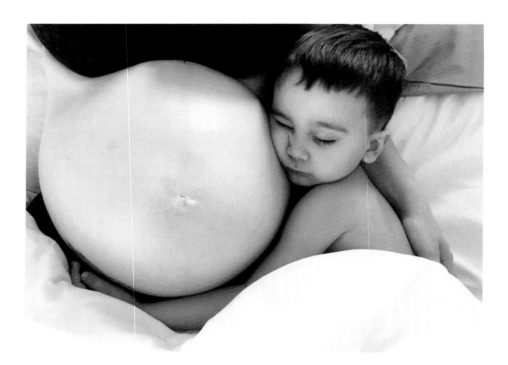

"Winston has always been a cuddler (and of course i am not going to complain) / but the need for him to cuddle grows greater as my belly grows bigger / today he fell asleep like this with his face smushed against my belly feeling his brothers kicks / before he fell asleep he said "mommy i think he is cute" / i hope their bond stays this strong outside the womb."

KELLY, 29 weeks
Findlay Ohio, USA

"Dear little love / i will hold you and rock you to sleep for as long as i can / which i hope is forever."

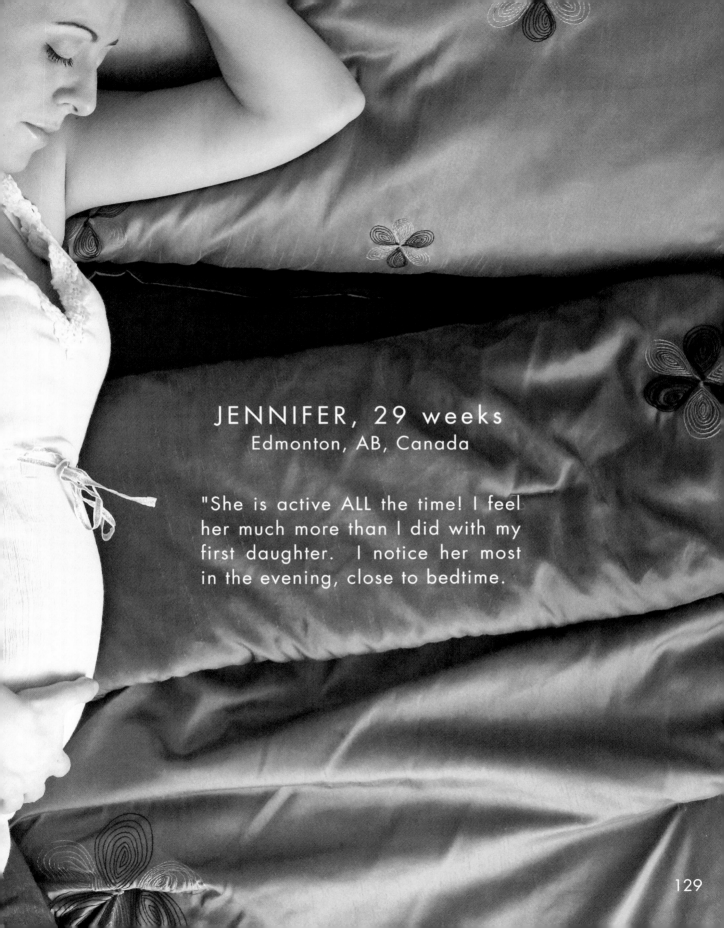

JENNIFER, 29 weeks
Edmonton, AB, Canada

"She is active ALL the time! I feel her much more than I did with my first daughter. I notice her most in the evening, close to bedtime.

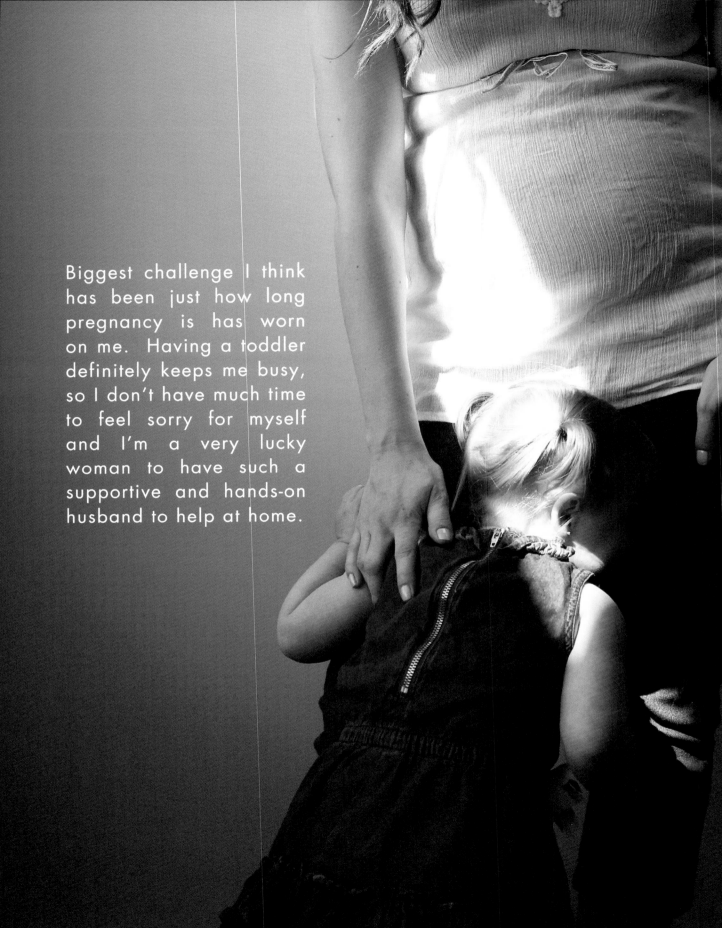

Biggest challenge I think has been just how long pregnancy is has worn on me. Having a toddler definitely keeps me busy, so I don't have much time to feel sorry for myself and I'm a very lucky woman to have such a supportive and hands-on husband to help at home.

My favourite part of being pregnant so far has been preparing for her arrival and knowing how great the end result is. I had a difficult first pregnancy, but if I had known how great our first daughter would be, I think it would have been more manageable. This time around I haven't felt as sick, so I have had fun preparing for her and getting her nursery ready, etc. Plus pulling out some of Lily's newborn clothing brought back great memories!

Approaching my due date I am feeling great and ready for this baby. I feel more prepared after going through this once before."

• • • • •

#dearbabystories

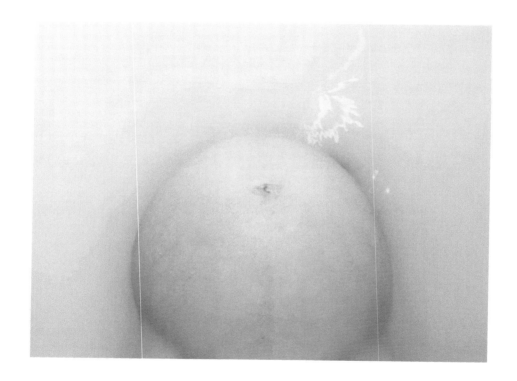

KELLY, 30 weeks
Findlay Ohio, USA

"I feel you always / every gentle nudge, every kick, every somersault / letting me know that in a few shorts weeks you will change all of our lives forever / i dream about you almost every night / your feet, your hands, your hair, but can never see your face / i can't wait until i can gaze upon you selfishly everyday."

CHARLOTTE, 30 weeks
Kuala Lumpur, Malaysia

"Mummy can we call my new baby sister Sleeping Beauty?"

• • • • •

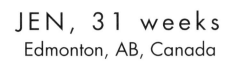

JEN, 31 weeks
Edmonton, AB, Canada

"I am excited to be her mother. One of my
core values is family and I think becoming
a mother will be deeply fulfilling.

When we actually started to set up her room, it gave me a bit of anxiety. Seeing her little clothes and crib made it more real for me. If something were to happen to her now, it would be devastating.

A couple of things have caught me off guard. I didn't realize that I would have such a strong reaction to my body changing.

It was different for me to see the beauty in my own pregnancy even though I could see it in others.

I didn't realize that my self esteem was tied so much to my flat stomach. Being pregnant, to me anyways, feels like your sex appeal is stripped away. I was surprised that it would bother me so much.

Another thing I wasn't prepared for is the feeling of isolation you get when you're pregnant. Not being able to do so much physically sets you apart from your friends. Playing it safe and not taking any physical risks (like cliff jumping on vacation) is a little boring and at odds with my personality.

One of my favorite moments was one day I was driving and she was moving around and, completely spontaneously, I blurted out, 'I love you.' And it was true. That moment was so special to me because I realized I loved my husband in the car driving as well. Something about Alberta skies and country music while driving lets me feel the most clearly.

There are some physical discomforts that aren't so nice, but honestly the hardest parts are emotional. Your feelings are all over the place because of your hormones. Trying to remember to be nice and stay positive when you are physically uncomfortable, sleep deprived and hormonal isn't easy.

First and foremost I want her to come out healthy and secondly I want her to feel happy and secure and loved. If she never goes a day in her life questioning if she is loved, I will feel like we did our job.

I think one of the biggest things I'm learning is just not to judge. Something about motherhood and pregnancy seems to give people the idea that they have free license to comment on others'. How about we all just give each other the benefit of the doubt? Let's support one another and respect everyone has different opinions and choices for what is best for them and their children."

• • • • •

KAYLEIGH, 32 weeks
Edmonton, AB, Canada

I hadn't really thought about this before until recently at 32 weeks. All of a sudden emotions took me over, and

I cried when I thought about how it wouldn't just be my husband and me anymore.

We have been married for 5 years, and all of a sudden I thought that we haven't had enough time! I know things will change when our baby comes, and we are both so excited, but I get moments where I'm overwhelmed with being greedy for time alone with just my husband before baby comes. Time is so precious, and it has gone by so fast. When we first found out I was pregnant, we thought, 9 months is a long time! Now that we only have 8 weeks to go, I have moments of panic, thinking, I want more time! Not that I don't want to meet our precious little one, but I also just want to cherish the last moments of just my husband and me... and to prepare more!

Right now, I worry most about tearing or ripping during labour... I feel good about the actual labour and delivery process except for that.

The hardest thing I have been dealing with is listening too much to other people and their opinions and ideas about what I need to do with my baby and products I need to have for it once it is born. In the first 2 trimesters I was feeling very good and prepared about having a baby and knowing what to do to care for it. I hadn't done any reading or really talked to many people about anything, I just felt like I would know what to do. However, recently people have been asking me so many questions about establishing sleep routines, when to introduce formula and bottles, etc., and I get overwhelmed thinking, I have no idea what I'm doing!!! I have always struggled with listening too much to what others say and feeling like I have to take their advice... my Mum has always been reassuring me that I will be a great mother and that I will know what to do, and to trust myself.

I feel like this is another step in my journey to gaining self-confidence and believing in myself and then giving the rest up to God.

I can't wait to see our baby's little nose and fingers and toes!!! I also look forward to the time where my husband and I will get to spend lying in bed with our baby and just snuggling and admiring it together."

• • • • •

#dearbabystories

TANYA, 33 weeks
Ann Arbor, Michigan, USA

"Dear baby girl, in just around 6 weeks we are due to meet each other on this side of earth. I'm learning you in a way already, but I can never picture your face, or your hands, or your hair...all I know is your sister's and it's hard to envision a whole new person. Today I've been emotionally drained, tearful, frustrated with this never-ending sciatic pain and lack of sleep over many months now. I've been impatient with your sister, harsh and irritated with your daddy, annoyed with the dog underfoot, lonely for friendships that seem to have faded, and overwhelmed by home and work and not enough time or energy to give to everyone. But, one thing that's always sure to bring me back to earth is feeling you move, as though you are gently reminding me from inside that you are here, always with me as we go, and it's going to be ok. I already love you more than you know, but I know not even as much as I will once you're in my arms. I don't want to wish time away with you safely inside, but I'm so ready for you. Dear baby, keep growing until you are ready, but please don't make us wait too long!"

KATYA, 33 weeks
Cabarete, Dominican Republic

"From the ancient times of cave women, it's through stories that we learnt, survived, and thrived as a species – we witnessed births of babies and birth of mamas. I didn't grow up that way. In my late twenties and happily pregnant for the first time,

I realized how embarrassingly little I knew about pregnancy and childbirth

– despite having doctors for parents, many great women in my life, and a BA degree. We all know how childbirth is portrayed on television: a woman's water breaks, she starts screaming in pain, everyone is freaking out, she gets rushed to the hospital, where doctors 'save' her and the baby. This just didn't seem right to me, and I became determined to fill in the gap. I started doing research and became obsessed with getting my hands on every book / documentary / teaching on natural childbirth I could find. It was AMAZING. The more I read, the more confident I felt about the way I wanted to bring our child into this world. At this point I must also mention how grateful I am for my amazing husband Rob – he eagerly read all the same books and watched all the same documentaries alongside me, supporting me every step of the way. Our lengthy discussions gave me strength and reassurance – I can do this."

• • • • •

JENA, 33 weeks
Minneapolis, Minnesota, USA

"Pregnancy number two has shown me that I really love being a mother. When I was pregnant with my first, there were so many unknowns and fears about what would happen, about my body, about if I could do it all. I've learned quickly that all of us moms are just trying to do the best we can with what we have and the children we are given. There's no secret sauce to this thing; it's really about learning more and more about who that sweet little baby you are raising is and doing your best to guide them into life. Realizing this has taken the pressure and edge off of me so much with the baby we are growing right now. I've taken all of those expectations off of him, and I am much more comfortable going with the flow of how things will turn out. I'm a middle child of 7 children, so I often run to my mother for advice.

I see myself learning from her that there's only so much you can truly prepare for or worry about. And some things like the 'perfect' way to raise your kids, or the 'perfect' answer – just don't really exist. I see myself realizing how laid back and wise she has become over the years by taking care of such a large family. I really lean on God's word for help in growing in this area and in guiding me to be the best parent I can be. Trusting Jesus and not worrying about tomorrow and believing things will work out for our good no matter what it looks like is what I set my sights on.

It doesn't always feel the easiest, but this is helping me raise my 2-year-old, and I know will be exactly my saving grace with our new addition. I'm excited for things to change, for our faces to light up even more the moment we meet him.

I'm excited to experience more unconditional love and understand true love even deeper.

I'm excited to see my daughter meet her brother, to watch their relationship grow. I'm excited to enter yet another world and layer of motherhood that some mothers will never know. Just like the first time around, I know it will be something new and at times challenging, but being a mom is something I know I was purposed to do. I'm excited for baby number 2."

• • • • •

VICTORIA, 34 weeks
St Albans, UK

"There were no harder words for me to digest than 'You have breast cancer' when I was 30 weeks pregnant. Instantly my main concern was my precious bundle that I'd been carrying and protecting for 6 months and what the next few months would have in store for us both. If it wasn't for my family and especially this beautiful face so excited to meet her sister to love and protect her like she now does so beautifully, life would have been a very dark place. Now my two gorgeous girls are keeping me strong and carry me through some gruelling and tough times. With the help of their love and beautiful smiles I'm now on the road to beating this."

• • • • •

AMY, 30 weeks
Texas, USA

"Being brave// I am amazed my body is capable of growing and comforting a tiny human
It doesn't have to be told what to do
You don't have to be told how to survive
We are in sync
You and me.
We share a bond
I can nourish you and your brother
Let those who worry do so for themselves
The three of us are content just the way we are"

#dearbabystories

"Being a mom has been the biggest blessing. It's given me a purpose, self esteem and so much joy. I do not want to imagine life with out my boys. Also I am going to miss this belly!"

NATALIA, 32 weeks
Vancouver, BC, Canada

"At the moment baby's movements feel like a disco full with dancing people.

The year when my first son was born was full of changes. My husband, who is working in soccer, got an offer from MLS, and we decided to come to Vancouver just 4 days before our son was born. My husband had to leave for Canada when the baby turned 3 weeks. And all the moving and paper work were on me. As well as the little angel. So I had just no time for any kind of postnatal depression, thoughts how our lives have changed or eating all the time. But that helped me realize very fast the actual needs of my baby, when he is crying for attention and when he is just hungry. This situation resolved me also from the baby pounds in less than 3 weeks. Of course it was not healthy, but stress can sometimes give a good kick for your metabolism.

My husband had enough things to deal with overseas, new job, new country, different language, preparations for our arrival. It was not always easy to keep the emotions calm. I spent our marriage anniversary as well as my birthday without him. And of course I got upset at that times. I am very grateful to my mother-in-law as well as to my friends in Germany who managed to find time to visit Berlin and to support me. Now we are in Vancouver for almost 1.5 years. And I would say it was worthy. Being in a foreign country all by ourselves without grand-parents or relatives who would be ready to have an eye on the little one any time or just to support you with wise words and a hug, pulled us tighter together. I would do it any time again. The only thing I would try to make better with the second baby would be to enjoy the first months of being a mom in a calm and relaxed atmosphere. At the moment I am trying to give all my attention to my son and to prepare our small family for the new member arrival.

My first was born in Germany, and the medical system there is really gorgeous. Except of the gender detection via ultrasound. They don't have the service of checking the baby's gender with the early blood test. At the fourth month the doctor told us, it will be a girl. And my husband was absolutely happy. My mother-in-law got everything in pink for the newborn.

But my inner feeling always said it is a boy.

Maybe because I wanted to have a boy. And during the 3D ultrasound at the end of the eighth month the doctor pointed on the curtain body part of the baby, letting us no more doubts that it is a boy! My husband was shocked and needed some time to get used to this new situation. And my mother-in-law had to bring all the purchases for the newborn back in store and exchange for the blue ones. And I was extremely happy! But when the baby came out all seconds thoughts were gone. And we pray to God every day and say thank you for this adorable little angel.

I would love to keep the gender of the second baby in secret. But I can give you a hint. My husband hopes that Canadian doctors are better equipped and are more precise in their diagnoses.

I try my best to take more time for the realizing that I am carrying a new life in me and to talk more to the baby inside me. To take some time, not always hustling somewhere. But also introducing my older son to the changing situation. Though it is not that easy at the age of 18 months to make him understand that something new is coming into our lives.

The first pregnancy seemed to be so easy. I had more time for myself and could go to have a nap whenever I wanted. Now I have another person I have to give full entertainment, with toddler gymnastics, baby swimming classes, laugh and fun time with mama and just filling the usual daily needs of an 18-month-old curious boy!

I feel like our new family dynamic will be more intense. I will have to manage our daily routine in half the time I'm used to. But I am excited and very positive about that. I am very grateful to my caring husband who spends most of his free time with us and tries to make my current pregnancy as easy as possible. The best feeling you can get from a man is protection, which I'm blessed to experience every single day and I hope that together we will be able to get used to the new circumstances much faster."

• • • • •

REBECCA, 33 weeks
Edmonton, AB, Canada

"Pregnancy is one of the most beautiful things I have ever experienced. To know that our love has created the little fibers of your being is simply phenomenal. They say a mother's love is like no other, and this is something I've begun to understand more so throughout pregnancy. It's incredible to experience an overwhelming love for someone we haven't yet met."

"Anticipating this girl's arrival has been not like anything I've experienced before. I feel at this point that a newborn (with a toddler) will be easier than being pregnant.

NADIA, 36 weeks
Edmonton, AB, Canada

The anticipation and the strong desire to just not be pregnant anymore brings on a lot of thoughts of the labour and when it might start. My mind goes and goes, and I start to question myself. Like most days I am so exhausted by the end of the day that I wondered, does this reflect on my preparation for the birth? Like a not well-rested marathon runner?

Thank goodness for doulas, midwifes, and wise friends to shake your head back to reality. And reality is, as a dear friend reminded me:

'When it happens it happens and your job is to let it.'"

ROBYN, 37 weeks
Edmonton, AB, Canada

"My favourite has definitely been the kicking-- it makes the pregnancy real, and it feels so reassuring. At times it's hard not get fixated and poke around at my stomach if I don't remember feeling movement in the last half hour. I've been lucky the baby is very active.

The hardest thing about being pregnant so far has been knowing that what I'm doing and how I'm treating my body is good for my baby. I have a lot of energy and still cross country skiing, swimming and cross training. I have a hard time taking it easy, and I get told that I should slow down. My doctor says I can do what I did before as long as I feel good. I just have to trust my body. After I'm done an activity the baby kicks stronger then ever. It has also been hard to eat since my second trimester. There is so much pressure on my stomach it makes me sick if I eat a normal-sized meal. I still have lots of energy, and the baby is growing as expected, so I just have to trust that if I do what feels best baby will be ok.

"Probably like most moms,
I worry the most if my baby
will be born healthy."

Probably like most moms, I worry the most if my baby will be born healthy. My sister stopped kicking at 37 weeks after being completely healthy during the pregnancy. For unknown reasons, 90% of her blood volume returned to my mom. She had to go for an emergency c-section and my sister ended up with severe cerebral palsy. I also work at the Stollery Hospital and see the worst case scenario so often it's hard to not let it get in my head.

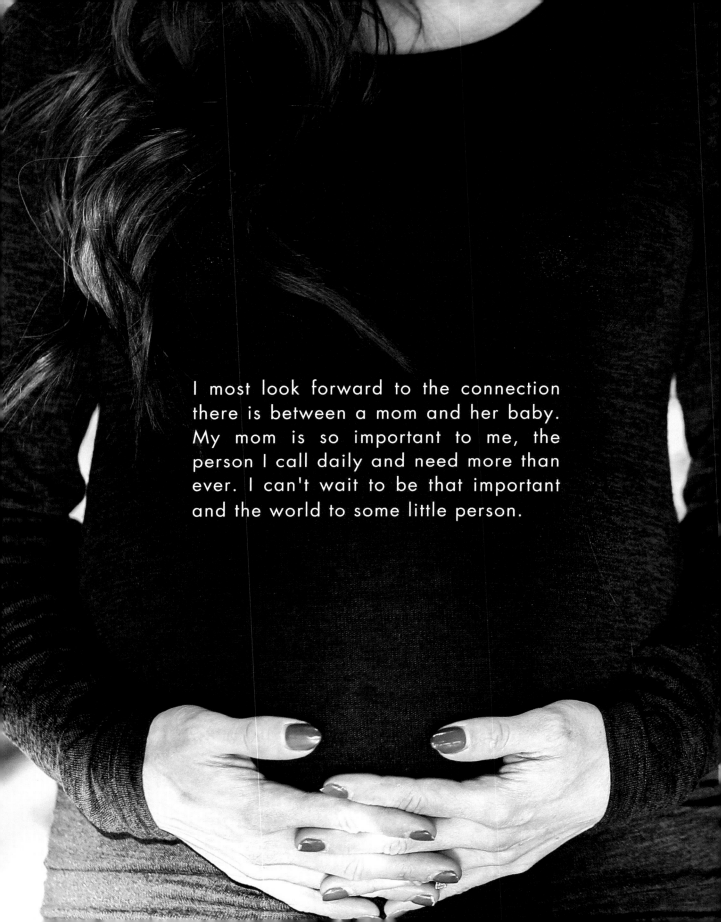

I most look forward to the connection there is between a mom and her baby. My mom is so important to me, the person I call daily and need more than ever. I can't wait to be that important and the world to some little person.

I think we will both be very active parents and start family adventures together early on.

I want our baby to feel safe and loved. To have a good example of a loving relationship that they are the product of. To feel like they can do anything and they can experience everything the world has to offer in its fullest."

· · · · ·

KAREN, 38 weeks
Vancouver, BC, Canada

"If you met me a year ago, there would be some similarities to who you would be meeting today. I would definitely not look the same. Our conversation would be very different. And for sure I'm mentally and emotionally very different. Life is ever changing realistically, and we can either update along with those changes or get stuck in our old patterns and 'ways.' I have always chosen to update. So here we are, well over a year later, and this is what I can share to date.

The last 8 months of my life have been all about learning how to LET GO all over again. And when I say LET GO, it's more than just one form of letting go.

Mentally: I had to let go of other people's STUFF.
I have had to learn how to let go of what other's think. I have had to learn how to let go of what other people will say or how they will react.

I have had to let go of fear.

And I have had to learn how to let go of something I have known for a good 30-plus years, my body!

As a dancer, dance instructor, and pilates instructor, that is something difficult to do, knowing all the 'what if's' that will happen on my insides and outsides. Books can scare the bejesus out us, and as women we have this concept of what beauty looks like based on a warped sense of reality put out there by magazines, Facebook posts, selfies, and so much more. It is toxic, the information that we are spoon fed over time and how it really creeps up on us in such a vulnerable time in our lives. All of a sudden we have known our bodies for 30-plus years as they are; mine literally has looked the same I feel like forever. . . we literally only can control the food we put it in this body during pregnancy and hope for the best.

We just pray that we don't get stretch marks because those won't look good in our bikinis anymore, and our man may get a wandering eye, or our boobs will get saggy after breastfeeding and then our perky boobs will be no more and that again may lead our man to a wandering eye. Even better!!!!! The whole peeing your pants thing. . . WOW. That is a scary one! Pelvic floor muscles really get tested during pregnancy. My scary 'ah ha' pelvic floor moment was when I was trying to get away with wearing regular jeans still and I was brushing my teeth. While I was leaning over the bathroom sink with my just-about-too-tight jeans on and the pressure of the button against my belly and my belly leaning over the edge of the sink I found myself about to cough and there was that moment. . . uh oh, did I just??? Wait. . . nope I didn't, I caught it, but that was a close call!!!! If there is any advice I can give to those who have not carried a baby yet in their beautiful belly, work on those muscles WAY BEFORE ever getting pregnant! I'm telling you that will save you in so many ways during pregnancy. You literally have to learn in a very fast amount of time how to allow yourself to let go of what was and step into the present reality of a changing body, a changing mindset, and a changing heart.

I'm on the biggest journey I have ever been on. The biggest ADVENTURE as I call it!!!!

From the moment I found out I had the opportunity to be a mother I felt so fortunate. It is something I have wanted for what feels like forever. And now it is here. And you will hear this from EVERYONE: there is no perfect time to have a baby. Really, there isn't. You know when it is right. And this is right for me, for sure.

There will always be stress: What about my business? What about my job? What about money? What about the cat? What about the insurance, and the next 20 years? Yeah. . . Well. . . . BILLIONS have done it with far less and have done it without books and have done it without a partner and have done it far from 'home.' Home is where the heart is, my friends. My heart is with me, my partner, and this baby, and that is where our home will be. For now the physical structure of a house is downtown Vancouver, but the heart that equals home is the group of us.

It is so true about the village effect. It takes a village to raise a child. Its not just a mom and dad, you know. I was so fortunate to have a village!!! My neighbours, my aunts, uncles, grandmas, cousins, friends, teachers, above all my mom and dad and my sister, but they needed support too, and that's what the village is for. So as we near the birth of this precious little angel that chose us, I find myself being pulled in the direction of where I have felt the village the most.

Although at times the village sometimes feels like it is not in this city at all.

Coming from Long Island, NY where my family still resides, and I have a sister with 2 boys of her own, I feel this huge push to figure out a way to get closer, to get back that way, to make sure we are all a part of this life together, rather than just touching base on the phone once a week or twice a week, where we only physically see each other in person twice a year. That is clearly not enough.

And then the next fear sinks in. . . . . What will one do for work? Medical insurance? Working visas? YADA YADA YADA. . . .

Gosh we can make ourselves literally go CRAZY!!!!!

On a daily basis I decide to take a deep breath, have some quiet time, and reflect on how I have gotten through all the other slightly heavy moments in life. The best way I know how is through movement. So I dance! I sway. I rock. I roll. I circle my hips through space. I stretch. I focus on my insides and feel my way through. I breathe. I move. I unleash. This beautiful little being inside of me moves with me.

This has by far been so amazing to feel the baby's movement and how it is similar to mine and how it differs from mine. What music the baby reacts to and what hands and food. This little angel is going to be aware, and I look forward to watching her intentions, intuition, and dreams develop. I can only imagine the amount of love that will come as soon as this baby is born."

• • • • •

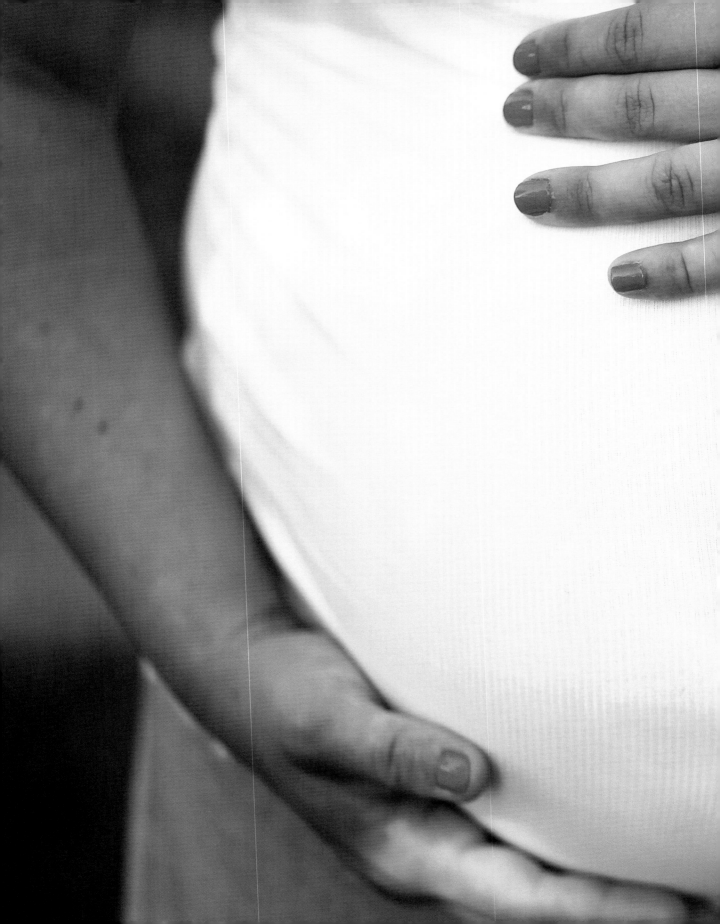

CARLING, 38 week
Edmonton, AB, Canada

"I really love the movements, in this pregnancy the baby is positioned with its little foot sticking out to the side of my belly! I love feeling the little foot move up and down the side of my belly!

My first pregnancy was healthy and free of complications. I feel like this pregnancy I have been much more laid back and trusting in my body and the changes that have happened and continue happening... our bodies can do pretty incredible things and I have trusted the healthy choices I make every day will help it manufacture a healthy and beautiful little person!

I most look forward to holding that tiny little human in my arms and dissecting their little features! I also can't wait for Jet to meet him/her, and see the interaction with him and his new little brother or sister!

Sleeping has always been difficult, especially in this last stage of pregnancy; I really struggle with moving from side to side in the night, and on some occasions the insomnia that comes with crazy hormone changes!

"In this last stage of my pregnancy, I have realized I am starting to become more and more anxious about the delivery; Jet had an extremely fast delivery, and I have noticed that lately I have become more and more anxious about this as the days go by and I get closer and closer to the end."

• • • • •

DANIELA, 38 weeks
Vancouver, BC, Canada

"I would not mind to wait more than 40 weeks if necessary to meet my baby. As much as I want to have my baby in my arms I love being pregnant and I really enjoy this big belly!

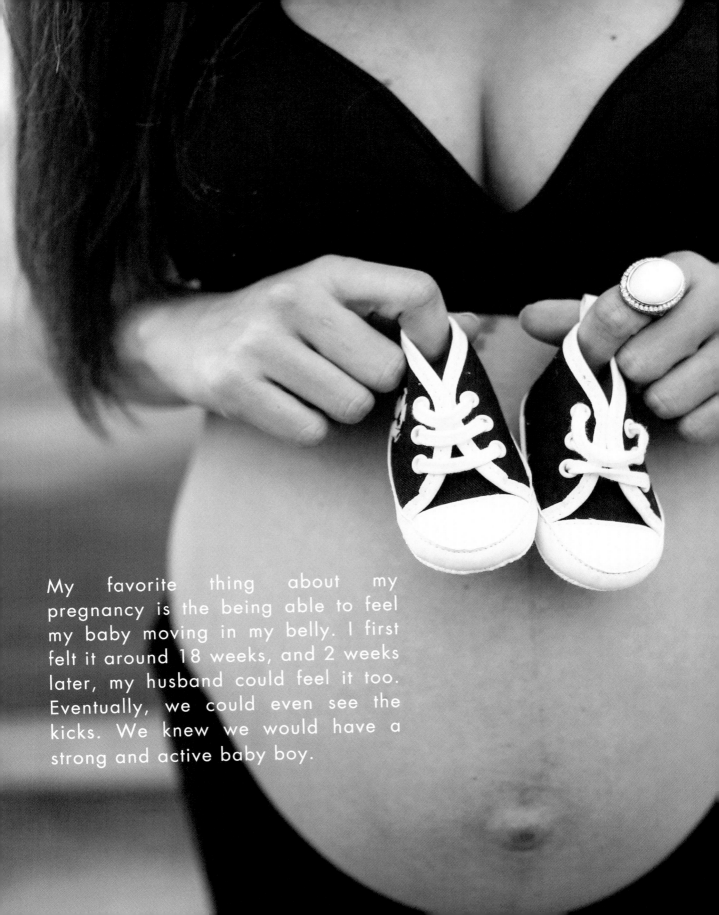

My favorite thing about my pregnancy is the being able to feel my baby moving in my belly. I first felt it around 18 weeks, and 2 weeks later, my husband could feel it too. Eventually, we could even see the kicks. We knew we would have a strong and active baby boy.

My second favorite thing definitely is the deep and restful sleep that I have had ever since the beginning of the pregnancy. I have always had some difficulty falling asleep, so being able to sleep in two minutes after laying down was like a dream come true! :) Summer started as I entered the third trimester of the pregnancy. Some days are very hot and a lot of people are asking me how I am feeling carrying this big, watermelon-shaped belly during the hot days but I guess the fact that I was raised in a hot country (Brazil) has helped me pass through this phase without complaints.

I constantly think of how my baby looks, whether he will have light or dark features, if he will be born bald or with hair, blue eyes like daddy or brown like mommy. Every time that I think about how my baby looks, I always picture a big baby! I can't stop thinking about the moment that I'll hold him in my arms, close to my chest and smell him. So many times, I have just ached to hug him! I already love him and miss him so much without even having met him.

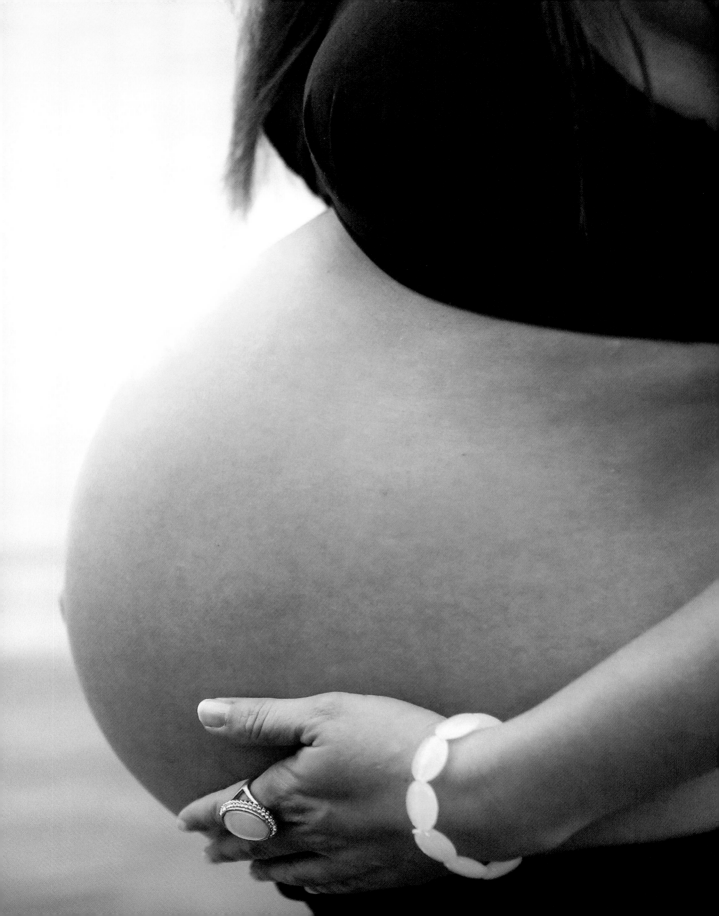

My biggest worry has always been about his health and well being. During the first 3 months, I was concerned about having a miscarriage. Then, as the pregnancy has progressed, I have been thinking about the baby's development and growth and now towards the end of my pregnancy, I don't want him to be born premature. I now realize that I will be always worried about something, no matter how old he is, just because he is and always will be the most precious thing in my life."

• • • • •

#dearbabystories

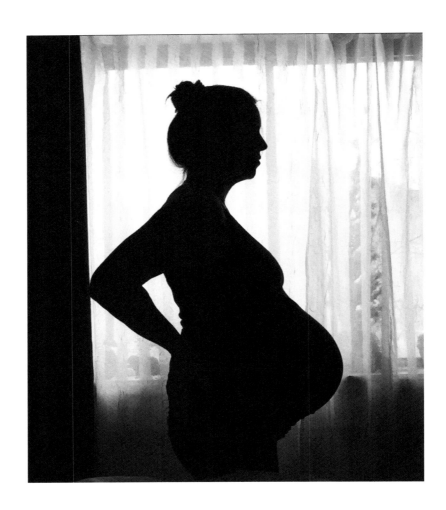

TANYA, 40 weeks
Ann Arbor, Michigan, USA

"Full term. Due date arrived. Officially late after today. I'm emotional and uncomfortably large and still having sciatica constantly. I've been tearful every day for the the past several. To say the end of this wait is glamorous would be a huge lie...I'm irritated with anyone who looks at me the wrong way, and the only thing I want is you in my arms instead of inside. I'm trying to embrace the power of the events that have yet to bring you earthside...but I keep meeting that with anxiety and fear instead of peace and strength and confidence. I'm hopeful we meet you in a matter of hours or days...not weeks yet. I need to see you soon."

LINDSAY, 40 weeks
Edmonton, AB, Canada

"Well, today is my due date. And I am still pregnant. No sign of baby's arrival. I am trying to stay calm and confident, and not give way to anxiety.

Fill me with your Holy Spirit Lord. I surrender all to you. My plans, my birth plan, my child, my body, my labour and delivery, my ideals, my will. I lay them at your feet, knowing you are and always have been, in control. Please Lord, hear my prayers. If it is your will, bring on my labour."

JOANNA, 40+ weeks
Edmonton, AB, Canada

"My overdue body is probably a reflection of my hearts concerns over my ability to be the mother I want to be. Will I be enough?"

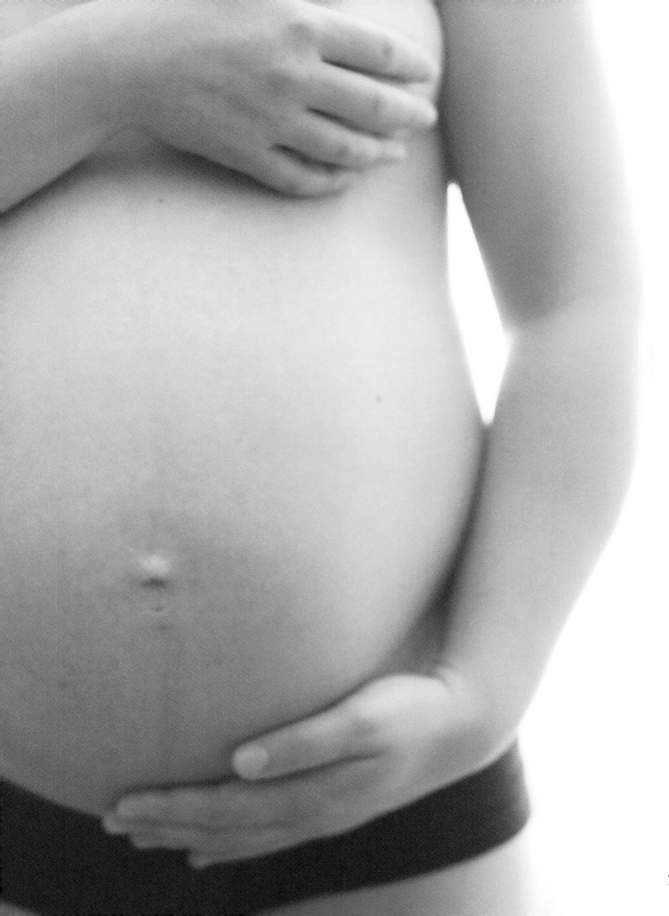

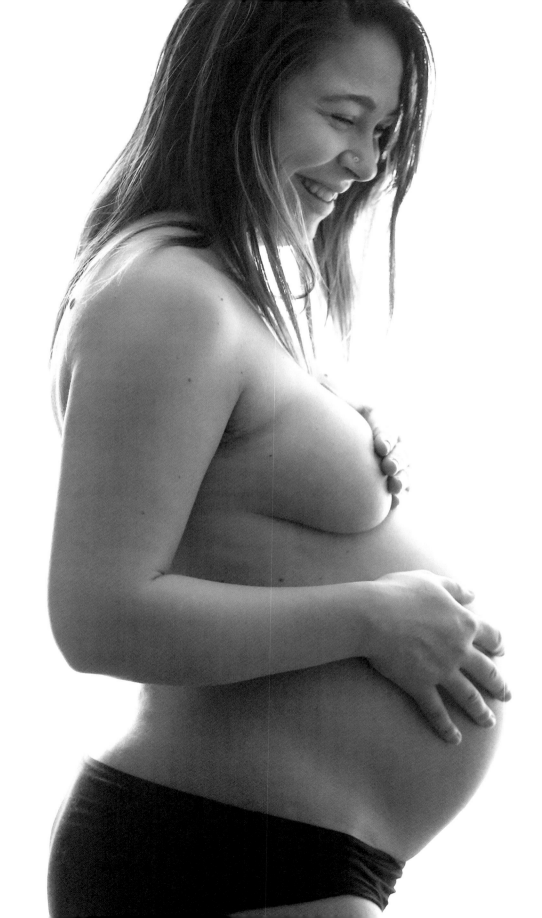

"All through my pregnancy I wasn't too concerned about going overdue, until I hit about 39 weeks and people who I never even spoke to starting coming out of the woodwork to ask me if I had had the baby yet. I'm 40weeks + 3 today and to be honest, I'm tired, mentally and physically, and when he moves it causes a lot more discomfort than I expected. His head smashes against my cervix many, many times a day, and it takes my breath away. I wake about 5 times a night to use the washroom. Every night I go to bed wondering if this will be the last night it is just myself and my husband - and the dog of course. I am left with my own impatience, not only for not knowing when labor will begin, but how it will begin, how it will progress and how I will cope. I have never felt so sure that I am so poorly prepared for parenthood, even though I have 'prepared' as much as possible, is there really such a thing? My overdue body is probably a reflection of my hearts concerns over my ability to be the mother I want to be. Will I be enough?"

• • • • •

BETHANY, 41+ weeks
Lancaster, PA, USA

"We're going into the hospital today. You'll stay with Nana and Pap-pap tonight, your first sleepover. I know you'll do great. The doctor says your baby sister is pretty big, and it's about time for her to come on out and meet you. I just know you're going to be an amazing big sister. I'm so ready for this little one to come yet I can't help but feel just a little sad. All kinds of sentimental. This is the last day of just you. It's been just you these last three years. You made me a Momma, you've taught me so much. There are so many bittersweet emotions going through my head and heart right now. So I'll take one more photo - because that's how I process, that's how I remember. This photo will forever be a reminder of all the memories we've had, just you and me, and all the wonderful new ones we are going to make as three."

Stories Index

Smile upon these blessed babies of courageous women who shared their stories. Also, thinking of and sending love to the angel babies that grace the pages of these stories and will forever be in our hearts.